TREASURY OF LITERATURE

PRACTICE BOOK

SIDEWALKS SING

HARCOURT BRACE & COMPANY

Orlando Atlanta Austin Boston San Francisco Chicago Dallas New York
Toronto London

CONTENTS

Printed in the United States of America

ISBN 0-15-301291-9

16   030   03 02 01 00

Name_____

Read each sentence and the words below it.

Write the word that best completes the sentence.

1. The coach told all the players to run around the _____ .

first   field   fork

2. Then the coach said, "It is time to _____ catching."

part   price   practice

3. "I feel _____ of the ball," thought Rod.

fix   fried   afraid

4. "It is your _____ to catch, Rod," called the coach.

turn   tune   torn

5. Rod _____ his eyes and held out his mitt.

cold   sold   closed

6. He _____ the ball drop into his mitt.

hat   heard   hard

Name_____

Think about what happened in "Ronald Morgan Goes to Bat." Fill in this chart about the story.

Who: Ronald Morgan

Where: baseball practice

Problem: He doesn't know how to play baseball.

How can you tell? _____

_____

_____

_____

Solution: _____

_____

_____

Finish the sentence.

"Ronald Morgan Goes to Bat" is about a boy who learns _____

_____

Name_____

Read each sentence. Add a time-order word
to each sentence to complete the story. The
words in the box may help you.

First	Later	Next	Then	Today

☆ 1. _____**Yesterday**_____ , Lilly had a great time at baseball practice.

2. _____ , she talked with all her friends.

3. _____ , she went to bat and hit the ball!

4. _____ , she pitched the ball to the other players.

5. _____ , Lilly rode home with one of her friends.

6. _____ , Lilly and her friends will practice again.

Name_____

Circle the naming part of each sentence. Then think of your own words to take the place of the naming part. Rewrite the sentence.

1. Baseball is a great game.

_____

2. Our pitcher throws very fast.

_____

3. That tall girl is our catcher.

_____

4. My brother plays third base.

_____

5. Felice and I stand in the field.

_____

Name_____

Read the story. Then answer the questions.

The Tigers got ready for their big baseball game.
First, all the players pulled on their team shirts.
Next, they all put on their team hats. Then, the
coach talked to the players about playing their best.
After the coach finished, everyone jumped up and
shouted, "GO, TEAM, GO!"

1. What is the first thing the Tigers do to get ready? _____

   _____

2. What word tells you this? _____

3. What do the Tigers do right after they pull on their team shirts?

   _____

4. When does everyone jump up and shout? _____

   _____

SUMMARIZING
the **LEARNING**   Noticing the _____ of events in a story
                can help you understand the story.

Name_____

Read the story and the questions beside the story. Then write the questions where they belong on the chart on the next page.

Is this a story to read for fun?

One time we chose teams for kickball at school. Could this story be about that?

Choosing Teams

Is Ms. Kwan a teacher?

"All right, class," Ms. Kwan said. "Soon we will start playing baseball. Today we will choose teams."

"Oh no!" thought Mandy, "I'm no good at baseball. No one will pick me. Why do we have to choose teams?"

Mandy looked around the room. No one else seemed worried.

"First, we will choose two team leaders," said Ms. Kwan. "On a slip of paper, write the name of one person who will be a

good leader. You don't have to pick someone who is good at hitting and throwing. Pick someone who can help the team." Mandy wrote the name of her best friend, Maria.

Then Ms. Kwan counted the votes. After she finished, she said, "Our new team leaders are Alex Morgan and Mandy Jones."

Mandy could hardly believe it! "I guess I'll be on a team after all," she thought.

When have I felt worried like this?

Who will be the leaders?

Was the story about what I thought it would be about?

Do I understand what Ms. Kwan told the class?

Would I like to read another story about Mandy?

GO ON

Name _____

Questions to Ask Before Reading	Questions to Ask During Reading	Questions to Ask After Reading

SUMMARIZING the LEARNING   You can help yourself read better by asking
yourself _____ before, during,
and after you read.

Name_____

Fill in the squares in this sidewalk game. Read the meaning inside each square. Then find the word that fits that meaning. Write the word inside the square.

Name_____

Think about what happened in "Matthew and Tilly." Fill in this web to show some of the things the two friends did together.

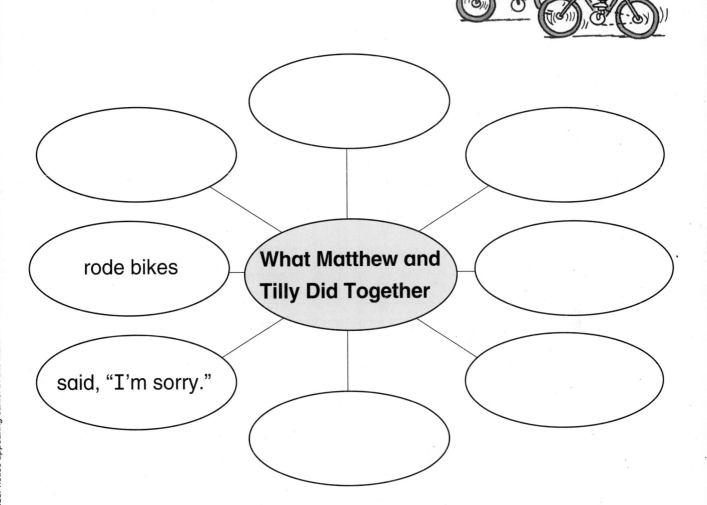

rode bikes

What Matthew and Tilly Did Together

said, "I'm sorry."

Write a sentence to tell why you think Matthew and Tilly are friends.

_____

_____

Name_____

Read the word under the first picture. Under the second picture, write a word that means the opposite of the first word. Choose words from the box.

brave	friends	old
smiled	together	upstairs

1. enemies _____

2. frowned _____

3. scared _____

4. downstairs _____

5. brand-new _____

6. apart _____

HBJ material copyrighted under notice appearing earlier in this work

Name_____

Underline the telling part of each sentence.
Then think of your own words to take the place
of the telling part. Rewrite the sentence.

1. My favorite sidewalk game is hopscotch.

_____

2. My friends and I play after school.

_____

3. Last night's rain washed away the lines.

_____

4. Barb drew the squares again.

_____

5. She is a good hopscotch player.

_____

Name_____

Read the story. Write the meaning of each underlined word. Then write the clue or clues that helped you figure out the meaning.

My sisters are great at playing jump rope. They swing two ropes at the same time. One day Charmaine asked me, "Do you want to try jumping?" I was very happy, because I have always wanted to try.

"I'd be thrilled!" I said.

Meaning: _____

_____

Clue: _____

_____

_____

_____

Charmaine said, "Let me demonstrate." Then she showed me how to run in while the ropes are moving. She showed me how to jump over one rope and then the other.

Meaning: _____

_____

Clue: _____

_____

_____

GO ON

Name_____

"Are you ready to try?" Charmaine asked me.

I nodded. Then I ran as fast as I could into the turning ropes. What a mess! The ropes and I got all tangled. One rope was wrapped around my arm. The other rope was twisted around my leg.

Meaning: _____

_____

_____

Clue: _____

_____

_____

"Don't be so hasty," Charmaine told me. "You don't have to be fast to get in. It's more important to be careful. Now, are you ready to try again?"

Meaning: _____

_____

_____

Clue: _____

_____

_____

SUMMARIZING the LEARNING How can you figure out the meaning of a new

word? _____

_____

Structural Analysis
and Contextual Clues   **13**

Name_____

Read the story. Think about what happens and why these things happen. Then answer the questions.

Tomorrow is Tilly's birthday, so Matthew wants to find a gift for her. First, he sees a jump rope that he knows Tilly would like. It costs too much money, though, so Matthew does not buy it. Then, Matthew sees a pretty little doll. Matthew knows that Tilly doesn't play with dolls, so he does not buy it. At last, Matthew sees a box of colored chalk. "This will be great!" Matthew thinks. "Tilly can use this chalk to draw some new sidewalk games." Matthew hurries to the counter to buy the chalk.

1. Why does Matthew want to buy Tilly a gift?

_____

2. Why doesn't Matthew buy the jump rope?

_____

3. Why does Matthew buy the box of colored chalk?

_____

••

SUMMARIZING
the **L**EARNING   When you read a story, you should think about

what happens and _____ things happen.

Name_____

Read each part of the story. Answer the questions.

Tilly is very excited about the gift from Matthew. First, she looks at the gift from every side. Next, she moves it from one hand to the other, trying to feel how heavy it is. Then, she holds it up to her ear and shakes it. At last, she yells, "Yes! It's chalk!" Then, she rips the paper off the gift.

1. What does Tilly do first? _____
2. What does Tilly do after she moves the gift from hand to hand?

_____

Tilly has lots of fun with her new colored chalk. First, she draws a brand-new sidewalk game. Then, Tilly makes lots of price tags. She and Matthew can use the tags when they play store. Then, she draws a big sign. It says, "Lemonade for Sale." Finally, Tilly uses her chalk to write a note. It says, "Thank you, Matthew."

3. What is the first thing Tilly does with the new chalk?

_____

4. What is the last thing she does with the new chalk?

_____

Name_____

Read each sentence. Write a word from the box to complete the sentence.

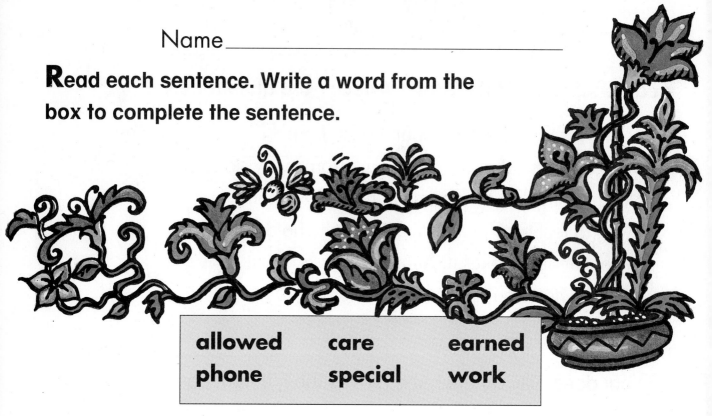

allowed	care	earned
phone	special	work

1. I picked up the _____ when it rang.

2. Aunt Jo asked, "Would you like to _____ for me?"

3. "Will you take _____ of my plants?" she asked.

4. Aunt Jo told me, "These are very _____ plants."

5. She said, "They must not be _____ to get dry."

6. I _____ two dollars for that job.

Name_____

Fill in this story map about "Arthur's Pet Business."

Beginning

Who is in the story?

When and where does the story take place?

What is the problem?

Middle

What important things happen?

Ending

How is the problem solved?

Write a sentence to answer the question.

How did Arthur show he is responsible? _____

_____

Name_____

Read each sentence. Finish the sentence
with a word that tells how the character
speaks. The words in the box may help you.

| answered | asked | explained | barked |
| ordered | promised | whispered | shouted |

1. "Will you look after my puppy while I go to the store?"

   Arthur _____ D.W.

2. "I won't be gone long," he _____.

3. D.W. _____, "Oh, all right."

4. "But come right back," she _____.

5. "I'm in charge of you now," D.W. _____ to the puppy.

6. "Woof," the puppy _____ back.

7. "I'm home!" Arthur _____ loudly as he opened
   the door.

8. D.W. _____, "Be quiet. The puppy is sleeping."

Name_____

Read each group of words. Write a sentence
that makes sense.

1. Neil   business   has   a   pet

_____

2. two   dogs   walks   he

_____

3. after   them   school   he   walks

_____

4. to   a   park   takes   he   the   dogs

_____

5. a   earns   dollar   Neil

_____

Name_____

Arthur wrote lists of names he might give his
new puppy. Write each list in alphabetical order.

1. Candy _____
   Buddy _____
   Edgar _____
   Doggo _____

2. Uncle _____
   Tex _____
   Sly _____
   Rover _____

3. Perko _____
   Pinky _____
   Pudge _____
   Pal _____

4. Sporto _____
   Silver _____
   Sandy _____
   Sunny _____

5. Daffy _____
   Darby _____
   Dash _____
   Dandy _____

6. Trumpy _____
   Trooper _____
   Trixie _____
   Tramp _____

Name_____

Read about each book. Then write <u>fiction</u> or
<u>nonfiction</u> to tell which kind of book it is.

1. Tiger Trainer

This book is about a real animal trainer.
The trainer works with tigers.

_____

2. How to Start Your Own Circus

This book tells how you and your friends
can start your own little circus. All you need
are some funny hats and a pet dog or cat.

_____

3. Ely & Edwin in the Big City

This book tells about two elephants who run
away from the circus. They move to the city
and open their own store there.

_____

4. Big-Top Bonnie

This book is about a girl who loves the
circus. She finds out that she can talk to all
the animals there, and they can talk to her.

_____

5. Clowning Around

This book is about circus clowns. It tells how
people learn to be clowns. It shows how
they put makeup on their faces.

Name_____

Read each book title and author's name. Think about how you would use a card catalog or a computer to find the book in a library. Write the letter you should use to look up the title and then the author.

1. Commander Toad in Space
by Jane Yolen

title _____   author _____

2. My Dog & the Knock Knock Mystery
by David A. Adler

title_____   author _____

3. Snakes Are Hunters
by Patricia Lauber

title _____   author _____

4. Ants Are Fun
by Mildred Myrick

title_____   author _____

5. Nate the Great
by Marjorie Weinman Sharmat

title _____   author _____

6. Fox on Wheels
by Edward Marshall

title_____   author _____

7. Here Comes the Strikeout
by Leonard Kessler

title_____   author _____

8. Arthur's Thanksgiving
by Marc Brown

title_____   author _____

Name_____

Read the story. Think about what happens and why these things happen. Then answer the questions.

Arthur was busy because he was taking care of Belinda's bullfrog, Henry's hamster, and Fredrico's fish at the same time. The fish needed more food, so Arthur asked D.W. to watch the pets while he went to the pet store.

"If you take too long, you'll owe me two dollars!" said D.W.

Arthur started to get onto his bike, but one of the tires was flat. So he had to walk all the way to the pet store. He quickly found the food on the shelf and went to pay for it. There were many people in line, though, so Arthur had to wait. Finally he paid for the fish food and left.

When Arthur got home, all of the pets were fine. "That will be two dollars," said D.W.

1. Why is Arthur so busy? _____

_____

2. What does Arthur's flat tire cause? _____

3. Why does Arthur owe D.W. two dollars? _____

_____

Name_____

Read the story. Think about the order in which things happen. Then answer the questions.

Some of my friends brought their pets to school today. First, Alice showed the class her little turtle. Its name is Pokey. Next, Ramon showed his pet rabbit, Flopsy. After the rabbit, we saw two cats. Trung and Nadia are the owners of the cats. The last pet was Yoko's big dog, Sport. We didn't have much time to see Sport because he raced right out of the room and down the stairs!

1. Who is first to show a pet to the class? _____

2. Which word tells you this? _____

3. Which pet is shown right after the turtle? _____

4. Which word tells you this? _____

5. When do Trung and Nadia show their cats?

_____

6. When does Yoko show her dog, Sport, to the class? _____

7. Which words tell you this? _____

Name_____

Read each sentence and the words below it.
Fill in the circle in front of the word that best
completes the sentence.

1. The baby ____ to everything we say.

　○ listens　　○ lists　　○ lost

2. This morning the baby was ____ the cat.

　○ took　　○ touching　　○ telling

3. Then the baby ____ to say a new word.

　○ learned　　○ looked　　○ living

4. I said, "Kitty, kitty," in a ____ voice.

　○ game　　○ going　　○ gentle

5. "I think the baby ____ that word!" I said.

　○ under　　○ upper　　○ understands

6. I didn't laugh, because I didn't want to hurt the baby's ____.

　○ feet　　○ feelings　　○ first

Name_____

Think about the two sisters in "I Have a Sister—My Sister Is Deaf." How are the two sisters alike? How are they different? Fill in this chart about the sisters.

Older Sister	Both Girls	Deaf Sister
is afraid of thunder	go to school	can't hear thunder so she's not afraid of it

Write a sentence that tells what the story is mostly about.

_____

_____

Name_____

Look at the pictures. What word tells the sound that goes with each picture? Write a sound word below the picture. Use the words in the box or other sound words you know.

| barking | knocking | purring |
| ringing | scraping | ticking |

1. _____ 2. _____

3. _____ 4. _____

5. _____ 6. _____

Think of other sound words. Without making any sounds, act out those words. Can your friends guess the words?

Name_____

Read each sentence. Write <u>statement</u> if the sentence tells something. Write <u>X</u> if the sentence does not tell something.

1. A deaf person cannot hear a whisper. _____

2. Can a deaf person feel my stamping? _____

3. My deaf friend watches TV. _____

4. How does she understand what is happening? _____

5. She looks at the picture and reads the words. _____

6. My friend likes to read and to play jump rope. _____

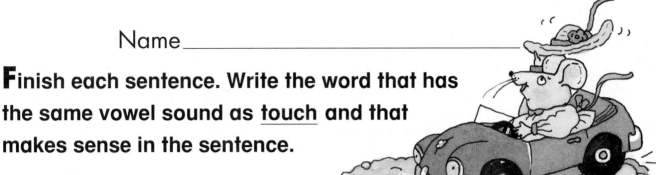

Name_____

Finish each sentence. Write the word that has the same vowel sound as <u>touch</u> and that makes sense in the sentence.

1. I'm on my way to visit my _____.

friend   cousin   young

2. She lives in a little house in the _____.

double   country   city

3. She is _____ than I am.

younger   older   touch

4. This road is pretty _____.

hilly   cousin   rough

5. When I hit the bump, my wheels didn't _____ the ground.

touch   rough   contact

6. I hope I won't have _____ with my car.

problems   rough   trouble

7. I hope she has _____ food for both of us.

more   couple   enough

Name_____

Read each question. Mark the best answer.

1. What should you find out before you start to study for a test?

   ○ Find out what the test will be about.
   ○ Find out what time the test will be.
   ○ Find out what your friend will study.

2. What should you do the night before a test?

   ○ Stay up late.   ○ Go to sleep early.
   ○ Watch a few movies.   ○ Watch TV for hours.

3. When you get a test, what should you do first?

   ○ Start writing the answers. ○ Talk to a friend.
   ○ Read a book.   ○ Read the directions.

4. Imagine that you are taking a test that you might not have time to finish. Which questions should you answer first?

   ○ the easy questions   ○ the hard questions
   ○ none of the questions   ○ your favorite question

5. What should you do when you finish your test?

   ○ Take a nap.   ○ Read the directions.
   ○ Check your answers.   ○ Talk to a classmate.

Name_____

Read each sentence and the words below the picture. Write the word that best completes the sentence.

1. I have a _____ craving for something to eat!

1. **tickle**   **time**   **terrible**

2. Here, Sir, taste this _____.

2. **soft**   **stew**   **stamp**

3. I don't like it! You must _____ for a rabbit to put in the stew.

3. **search**   **some**   **seven**

4. Just as he was about to grab his _____, the rabbit ran away.

4. **past**   **prey**   **pay**

5. Try this _____ stew.

5. **delicious**   **dark**   **day**

6. Ah, yes! Those carrots are _____ in the stew.

6. **party**   **penny**   **perfect**

Name_____

Think about what happened in the story. List
the events in order on the flowchart.

1. The wolf craved chicken stew.

2. The wolf went in search of a chicken.

3.

4.

5.

Write the most important thing that the wolf did.

_____

_____

Name_____

Read each sentence. Add a word that means the opposite of the word under the line. The words in the box may help you.

find	follow	help	little
sad	wrong	cry	

1. The wolf saw a _____ chick.
<u>big</u>

2. The chick looked _____ .
<u>happy</u>

3. The wolf wanted to _____ the chick.
<u>hurt</u>

4. "Is something _____ ?" the wolf asked.
<u>right</u>

5. The chick said, "I cannot _____ my mom."
<u>lose</u>

6. Then the chick began to _____ .
<u>laugh</u>

7. "I'll help," said the wolf. "Just _____ me."
<u>lead</u>

••• THE WOLF'S CHICKEN STEW •••

Name_____

Begin each question with a question word
from the box. Use the correct end mark.

Who	What	When	Where	How	Why

1. _____ is wearing the hat ____

2. _____ is the wolf holding ____

3. _____ did the wolf make the food ____

4. _____ are the chicks visiting the wolf ____

5. _____ do the chicks live ____

6. _____ will the food be cool enough to eat ____

Write your own question about the picture.

7. _____

Name_____

Read each sentence. Write the word that has the same vowel sound as <u>bird</u> and that makes sense in the sentence.

bird

1. It was the wolf's _____ party.

   second   first   shirt

2. The party was for her _____ .

   birthday   family   earth

3. She invited four of _____ best friends.

   our   dirt   her

4. The fox said, "I have _____ you like to read."

   seen   third   heard

5. "I had to _____ all over for this book."

   look   search   earth

6. "It looks _____ !" said the wolf.

   perfect   great   girl

Name_____

Read the beginning of the story. Then answer the questions.

    Mrs. Chicken had a birthday party for all her little chicks. Uncle Wolf came to the party, of course. Many other friends came to the party, too. The chicks and their friends played many games. Then Mrs. Chicken said, "All right, everyone. Please sit down at the table. We are ready for the best part of the party." She turned out the lights.

1. What do you think will happen next? _____

_____

2. What clues helped you figure out what will happen next? _____

_____

_____

_____

_____

SUMMARIZING *the* **L**EARNING   When you read a story, you can look for clues that will help you _____ what might happen next.

Name_____

Read the word meaning on each bat. Find the word in the box that goes with that meaning. Write that word on the ball beside the bat.

company	familiar	family
lose	realizes	world

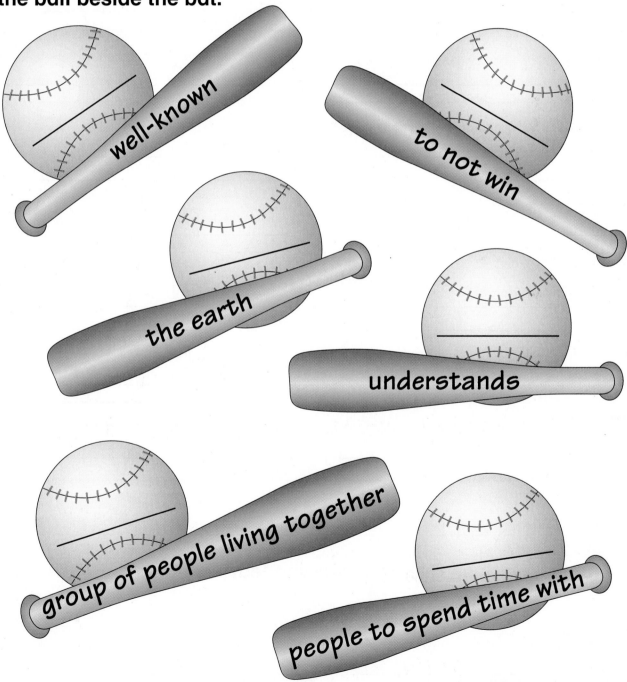

well-known

to not win

the earth

understands

group of people living together

people to spend time with

Name_____

Think about what happened in "Everett Anderson's Friend."
Why did each thing happen? Fill in this flowchart.

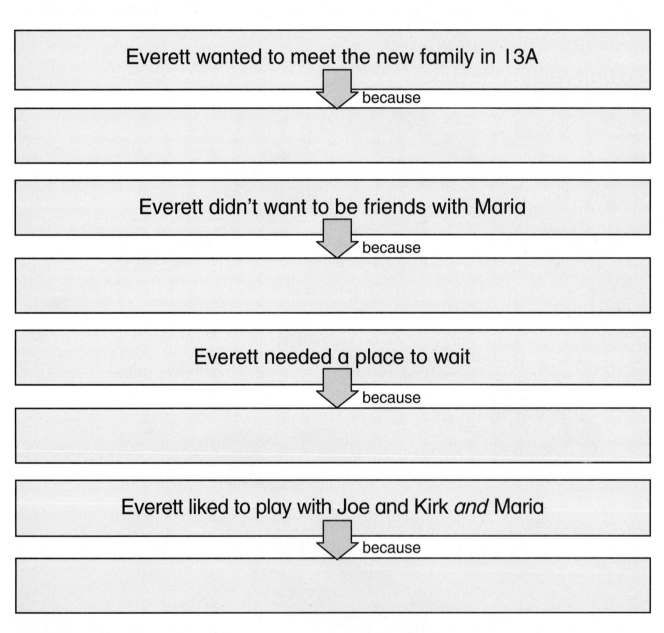

Everett wanted to meet the new family in 13A

▽ because

Everett didn't want to be friends with Maria

▽ because

Everett needed a place to wait

▽ because

Everett liked to play with Joe and Kirk *and* Maria

▽ because

What lesson does Everett Anderson learn?

_____

_____

Name_____

Read the first sentence in each pair. Then finish the second sentence. Write a word that rhymes with the word in dark print. You may choose a word from the box.

best	float	fun	places	wait

Look at my **boat**.

It really can _____!

Don't be **late**!

The train won't _____.

Let's stop and **rest**.

This bench looks _____.

We're starting the **races**.

Are you all in your _____?

Let's go and **run**.

It looks like _____!

ACTIVITY CORNER

Work with a partner. Together, write two or more sentences with rhyming words. Then draw a picture to go with your sentences.

Name_____

Read each sentence. Write <u>exclamation</u> or <u>command</u> to tell what kind of sentence it is. Then add the correct end mark.

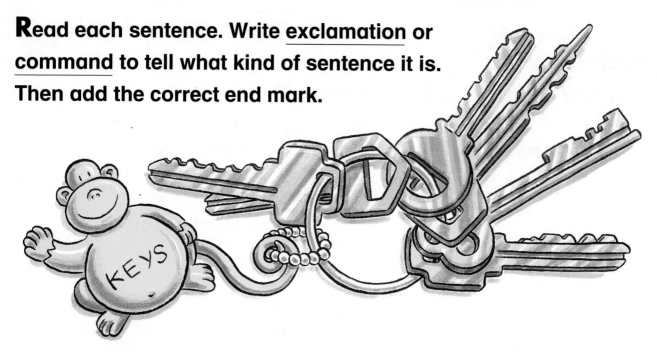

1. Don't lose this key ____   _____

2. Put the key in your backpack ____   _____

3. Please call me right after school ____   _____

4. Oh, no, we're locked out ____   _____

5. Hurray, I found the key at last ____   _____

6. Wow, you've got a lot of keys ____   _____

Write your own exclamation or command.

7. _____

Name_____

Piggly wants to invite Ronny Robin to do something fun. So she leaves clues for him. Read each clue. Write the word that has the same vowel sound as <u>fly</u> or <u>child</u> and that makes sense in the sentence.

fly   **child**

1. A rooster wakes _____ family every day.

                sky   your   my

2. The _____ farmer feeds the animals.

         busy   kindly   find

3. Is the barn _____ the farmhouse?

           by   cry   near

4. Ducks _____ over the pond.

         mind   soar   fly

5. The pigs live in a muddy _____.

                 sty   why   yard

What does Piggly want Ronny to do? Write the answers on the lines below to figure out the secret message.

_____	_____	_____	_____	_____
2	**4**	**3**	**1**	**5**

Name_____

Read the story. Then answer the questions.

Barney the Dancing Bear moved to the city. Each day he walked on sidewalks beside tall buildings, looking for a job. Nobody needed a dancing bear. He was so tired. He took off his hat and sat down on his old suitcase. Who might want a dancing bear?

There were so many people walking by! Sounds of cars, buses, and trucks filled the air. Just then he saw a sign, "*Bearly Dancing*—Tryouts for Dancing Bears." Barney jumped for joy!

Now, if you go to the city, it's easy to find Barney. He's on stage dancing in the famous show *Bearly Dancing*.

1. What is Barney like? Write some details. _____

_____

2. What is the city like? Write some details. _____

_____

3. Write some details that help explain what happens. _____

_____

SUMMARIZING
the **L**EARNING   Story details tell _____ is in a story,

_____ the story takes place,

and _____ happens.

Name_____

Everett Anderson listed the names of all his
friends. Rewrite each part of Everett's list.
Write the names in alphabetical order.

1. Mei _____

Molly _____

Margo _____

Miyoko _____

2. Shawn _____

Sergio _____

Susana _____

Sonja _____

3. Norm _____

Ned _____

Nan _____

Nina _____

4. Jesse _____

Jason _____

Jed _____

Jacob _____

5. Lulu _____

Lucia _____

Luis _____

Lumpy _____

6. Rocky _____

Ron _____

Rodney _____

Roberto _____

Name_____

Read each sentence. Write a word from the
box to complete the sentence.

through	package	answered
problem		gigantic

1. The doorbell rang, and Jeb _____ it.

2. On the steps was a _____ box.

3. "Is there a _____ of food or clothes inside?" Jeb
   wondered.

4. "Getting this into the house will be a _____," he said
   to himself.

5. "How can I get it _____ the door?" he wondered.

The work made Jeb so tired that he fell asleep!

Name_____

Think about Mitchell and Margo in "Mitchell Is Moving." What problems did they have? How did they solve their problems? Fill in this chart.

Old Place

Mitchell	Margo
Problem: was tired of his house	did not want Mitchell to go
Solution: planned to move	_____ _____

New Place

Mitchell	Margo
Problem: was lonely	missed her old neighbor
Solution: _____ _____	_____ _____

Write your own ending to this sentence.

"Mitchell Is Moving" is about two friends who _____

_____

Name_____

Read the first sentence in each pair. Then finish the second sentence. Add <u>un</u> to the word in dark print from the first sentence.

1. Mitchell tries to **lock** the box.

Margo tries to _____ the box.

2. Mitchell tries to **stick** a label to the box.

Margo tries to _____ the label.

3. Mitchell tries to **tie** a string around the box.

Margo tries to _____ the string.

4. Mitchell tries to **clip** the boxes together.

Margo tries to _____ the boxes.

ACTIVITY CORNER

With a partner, think of four other words that begin with <u>un</u>. Act out your words for the rest of your classmates.

Name_____

A. **R**ead each sentence. Underline each noun.
Then write the nouns on the chart. Add
more nouns.

1. Dinosaurs lived long ago.

2. Some had large tails and teeth.

3. Some lived near swamps and ate plants.

4. Others were as small as a chicken.

5. My mother and father took us to a museum.

6. We saw large bones and footprints in rocks.

Person	Animal	Place	Thing

**Nouns: People, Animals,
Places, Things**

Name_____

B. Complete each sentence by writing a noun that names a person, an animal, a place, or a thing.

7. Some _____ had sharp teeth and claws.

8. Did baby dinosaurs hatch from _____?

9. Flying dinosaurs had large _____.

10. _____ were the favorite food of many dinosaurs.

11. My _____ and I like tyrannosaurus rex the best!

12. I wonder if dinosaurs ever lived in a _____.

Nouns: People, Animals, Places, Things

Name_____

Read each sentence. Write a word from the box to finish the sentence.

bridge	edge	ice	lace
climb	race	thumb	

1. The _____ is thick enough for skating.

2. Let's skate all the way to the _____ .

3. Do you want to _____?

4. Wait for me! I have to _____ my skates.

5. I can't get my _____ into my mitten, either.

6. Would you please help me _____ down from the rock?

7. Let's skate to the _____ of the lake.

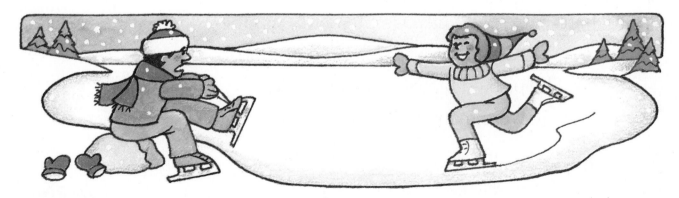

Name_____

Read each paragraph. Think about what the paragraph is mostly about. That is the <u>main idea</u>. Then write the sentence that tells the main idea.

The Clemsons are happy about moving. Mrs. Clemson likes the new house they will live in. She likes her new job, too. Richard has already seen his new school. He thinks it looks like fun. Julia is happy that she will be near Grandma Lou. Grandma Lou will take care of Julia while her mom works and her brother is at school.

1. What is the main idea? _____

_____

Everyone in the Clemson family worked hard to get ready for the move. Julia helped carry boxes into the house. She packed her toys. Richard packed clothes. He put books in other boxes. Mrs. Clemson put pots and pans into boxes. She packed plates and spoons, too. Soon there were many full boxes.

2. What is the main idea? _____

_____

Name_____

At noon, Richard and Julia made cheese
and tomato sandwiches for everyone. Mrs.
Clemson made some lemonade to drink. Then
the family sat on the porch and quickly ate their
lunch. The Clemsons were very hungry from all
the hard work they had done all morning.

3. What is the main idea? _____

_____

At the end of the day, Mrs. Clemson sat
down in her rocking chair. She put her feet up
on one of the boxes. Richard lay down on the
couch. Julia fell asleep on the floor. All the
Clemsons were tired from packing boxes.

4. What is the main idea? _____

_____

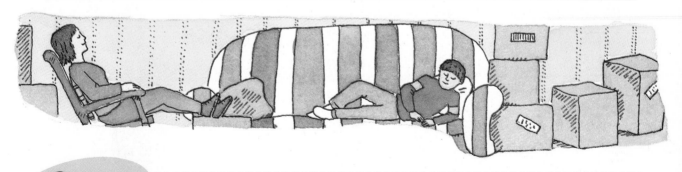

SUMMARIZING
the **L**EARNING   The details in a story or paragraph work

together to tell about the _____ idea.

Name_____

door

Finish each sentence. Write the word that has the same vowel sound as <u>door</u> and that makes sense in the sentence.

There must be _____
floor   forty   fifty
boats out on the lake!

Look how high my kite can
_____.
fly   roar   soar

We're getting too close to the
_____ !
shore   short   beach

I'm glad I _____ a jacket.
before   brought   wore

It's already _____ o'clock.
three   four   horn

Name_____

Read each paragraph. Think about why things happen. Then answer the question.

Mitchell got a postcard from his old friend Marvin. Marvin was coming for a visit because he missed Mitchell and Margo. Mitchell was glad that Marvin was going to come.

1. Why was Marvin coming for a visit? _____

_____

Mitchell was happy about the postcard. He wanted Margo to read it, so he ran over to her house. "Look, Margo!" he shouted. "I have a postcard from Marvin."

2. Why did Mitchell run over to Margo's house? _____

_____

Mitchell knocked on Margo's back door. There was no answer. He peeked in her windows. Margo was nowhere to be found. Then he went around to her front door and saw this note.

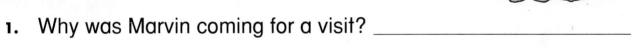

3. Why wasn't Margo at home? _____

_____

Name_____

Read each sentence and the words below it.
**Fill in the circle in front of the word that best
completes the sentence.**

1. We were ____ working in the yard all morning.
   ○ build   ○ best   ○ busy

2. I helped my dad ____ the broken fence.
   ○ real   ○ repair   ○ rest

3. I was unhappy because the hot sun ____ me.
   ○ bothered   ○ bringing   ○ brought

4. Then I saw my friend Jamal coming ____ my house.
   ○ toad   ○ toward   ○ truck

5. He ____ me a glove and asked me to play baseball.
   ○ tossed   ○ tossing   ○ topping

6. My dad is ____ . He said I could go since I had worked so hard.
   ○ from   ○ fist   ○ fair

7. My other friends were ____ at the park when we got there.
   ○ read   ○ already   ○ after

Name_____

Think about what happened in "Jamaica Tag-Along." Why did each thing happen? Fill in this chart about the story.

Jamaica wanted to play basketball because _____

_____

She followed Ossie to the court because _____

_____

Ossie sent her to the sandlot because _____

_____

When Jamaica met Berto, she didn't want

him near her at first because _____

_____

Jamaica decided to play with Berto because _____

_____

Answer the question.

What lesson did Jamaica learn in this story? _____

_____

_____

Name_____

Read each sentence. Think about the meaning of the underlined word. Then circle the picture that shows the meaning of the word.

1. I looked at my <u>watch</u> to see what time it was.

2. I still had time to <u>watch</u> the game.

3. I hopped off the <u>swing</u> and ran toward the basketball court.

4. I stood on the top <u>step</u> so I could see the players.

5. I saw Rita grab the ball and <u>shoot</u>.

6. The ball missed the <u>basket</u>.

7. Then I saw a player <u>step</u> on Rita's foot.

Name_____

A. Write each special name and title correctly on the name tag. Add periods where they are needed.

1. mr paco gonzalez

2. miss mary weiler

3. dr phyllis gold

4. ms rossi

5. mr jim marks

6. mrs brenda dennis

GO ON

Special Names and Titles of People

Name_____

B. **W**rite each sentence correctly. Add capital letters and periods where they are needed.

7. We live by dr and mrs chen.

_____

8. My friend greg smith lives upstairs.

_____

9. My mom works with mrs smith.

_____

10. maria gonzalez and I play together.

_____

11. mr jackson fixed the swings.

_____

Name_____

Read each sentence. Write the word that has the same vowel sound as <u>field</u> and that makes sense in the sentence.

field

1. The children were _____ working on their castle.

     still busy baby

2. They made _____ people to go into the castle.

    little tiny any

3. They used _____ of paper to make flags.

    pieces field bits

4. "It looks so good, I can almost _____ it is real."

    think believe chief

5. "I hope _____ steps on it," said Taro.

   no one nobody funny

6. "We won't let _____ do that," said Jason.

    them icy anyone

Name_____

Read the story. Think about what happens in
the beginning, the middle, and the ending.
Then answer the questions.

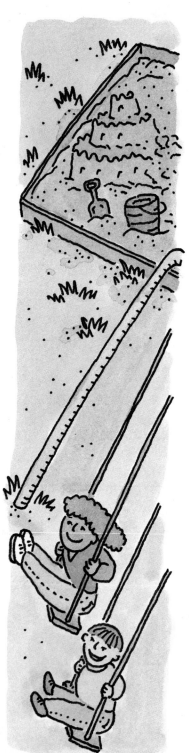

One day Tanya had no one to play with.
Her friends were all busy. So Tanya went to the
park. She hoped that her friend Jimmy would
be there. Maybe he would build a sand castle
with her.

When Tanya got to the park, Jimmy *was*
there! He was swinging, and he looked very
happy. Tanya asked Jimmy if he wanted to build
a sand castle. But Jimmy shook his head and
went on swinging. Tanya started to dig in the
sand. She worked hard on her castle. She kept
waiting for Jimmy, but he was too busy
swinging. Tanya felt lonely. She was not having
much fun.

After a while, Tanya went over to Jimmy.
"Do you want me to push you?" she asked.

Jimmy nodded happily. So Tanya pushed
Jimmy in the swing. Then she got onto the
swing next to him and started swinging, too.
Now she and Jimmy were both having fun!

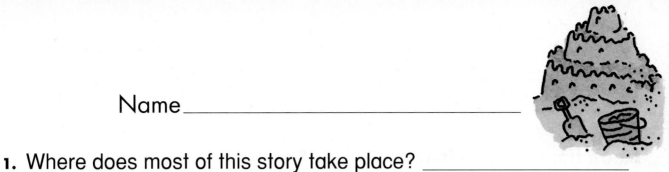

Name_____

1. Where does most of this story take place? _____

_____

2. What happens in the beginning of the story? _____

_____

_____

3. What happens in the middle of the story? _____

_____

_____

_____

_____

4. What happens at the end of the story? _____

_____

5. What is a different ending the story could have had? _____

_____

SUMMARIZING
the **L**EARNING   A good story has a <u>beginning</u>, a _____,

and an _____ .

Name_____

Read the meaning in each cloud. Then find the
word that goes with that meaning. Write that
word on the cloud.

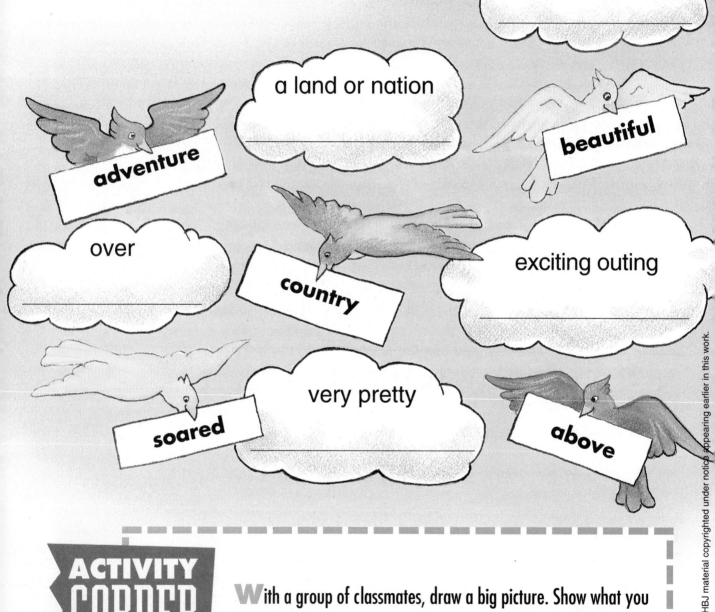

flew high
_____

a land or nation
_____

beautiful

adventure

over
_____

country

exciting outing
_____

soared

very pretty
_____

above

ACTIVITY CORNER

With a group of classmates, draw a big picture. Show what you
would like to see if you could soar in the sky.

HBJ material copyrighted under notice appearing earlier in this work.

Name_____

What do Rosalba and Abuela see as they fly over the city in "Abuela"? Fill in the missing parts of this web about the story.

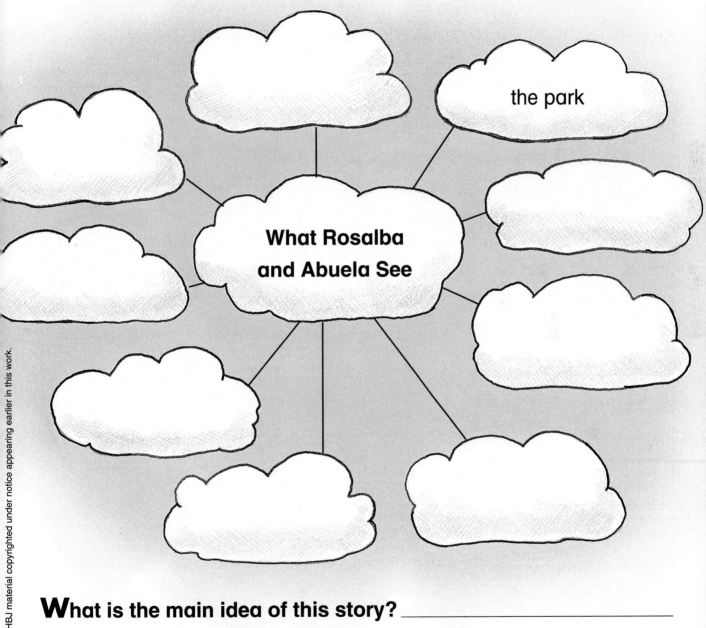

the park

What Rosalba and Abuela See

What is the main idea of this story?_____

_____

Name_____

Read the words in the box. They are all
Spanish words used in English. Write each
word below the picture it names.

| bananas | burros | mangos | patio | rodeo |

1.

_____

2.

_____

3.

_____

4.

_____

5.

_____

Name_____

A. **R**ead the sentences below. Circle the words that name special animals or places. Rewrite the proper nouns. Use capital letters where needed.

1. The lincoln memorial is tall. _____

2. Our dog rover walks with us. _____

3. Did you visit orlando, florida? _____

4. The potomac river is very wide. _____

5. We landed at freedom airport. _____

6. Salt lake city is far from here. _____

Names of Special Animals
and Places

65

Name_____

B. Write each sentence correctly. Add capital letters where they are needed.

7. Last fall, we visited chicago.

_____

8. We left our cat, fluffy, at home.

_____

9. I rode a bike in lincoln park.

_____

10. We went to the top of the sears tower.

_____

11. We stayed at the park view inn.

_____

Name_____

Read each sentence. If it tells about things that can happen in real life, write <u>Real</u> on the line. If it tells about things that are make-believe, write <u>Make-believe</u>.

_____ 1. Both boys flapped their arms and started to fly through the air.

_____ 2. The plane flew right through the clouds.

_____ 3. The cat jumped onto Grandma's lap and began to purr happily.

_____ 4. The cat stared at Grandma and asked, "Isn't it about time for dinner?"

_____ 5. Reggie raised his hand again, but the teacher called on someone else.

_____ 6. Since Reggie was the size of a mouse, he was able to hide behind the teacup.

_____ 7. The big gray horse talked it over with the cows, but no one knew what to do.

_____ 8. Gemma put her saddle onto the big gray horse and led him out of the barn.

SUMMARIZING *the* **L**EARNING Some stories tell about things that are <u>real</u>.

Some tell about things that are _____.

Name_____

Read the words in each box. These are entry words on a dictionary or glossary page. Write the words in alphabetical order. Then circle the two guide words for that page.

awake	already	answer	believe
after	allow	afraid	bark

1. _____   5. _____

2. _____   6. _____

3. _____   7. _____

4. _____   8. _____

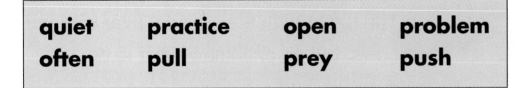

quiet	practice	open	problem
often	pull	prey	push

9. _____   13. _____

10. _____   14. _____

11. _____   15. _____

12. _____   16. _____

Name_____

Read the glossary page below. Then answer the questions.

---

special   **terrible**

spe • cial   Extra nice; different from   **taught**   Helped someone learn
                 the others: **Pam wears**   something: **The**
                 her *special* **dress on**   **dentist** *taught* **us**
                 holidays.   **how to brush our**
                                                                  teeth the right way.

stay   To live somewhere for a
                 while; not to move or go   **ter • ri • ble**   Very big; great: **Anita**
                 away: **We will** *stay* **at**   **had a** *terrible* **need**
                 the beach house all   **for a drink of water**
                 summer.   **after running the**
                 syn. remain   **race.**

stew   A thick soup: **We ate**
                 stew **made with meat,**
                 potatoes, and carrots.

---

1. What are the guide words? _____

2. What is the second entry word? _____

3. What does <u>taught</u> mean? _____

4. What does <u>terrible</u> mean? _____

5. Which word means "a thick soup"? _____

6. What is another word that could be on this page? _____

Name_____

Read each sentence. Write the word that has
the same vowel sound as either <u>hair</u> or <u>deer</u>
and that makes sense in the sentence.

hair

deer

1. Ted and Ed _____ a tent.

have   care   share

2. "Do you _____ a strange sound?" asks Ed.

hear   spear   notice

3. "Could there be a _____ in the woods?"

fox   bear   wear

4. Ted says, "I think it's just a _____."

cheer   deer   boy

5. He adds, "Maybe it's just a _____ of mice."

couple   chair   pair

6. "Do you _____ to go outside and see?" Ed asks Ted.

want   hair   dare

Name_____

Read each sentence. Write a word from the
box to complete the sentence.

caught	different	discovered	lived	owners

1. Bubbles _____ in a big glass bowl.

2. Bubbles had two _____, twins named Ella and Bella.

3. The twins looked alike. Bubbles knew they were _____.

4. Only Ella fed Bubbles. When Ella _____ a bad cold,
   Bubbles worried about his dinner.

5. With luck, Bubbles _____ a new way to get his dinner.

Name_____

Fill in this chart about "Six-Dinner Sid." Finish the sentence in each box.

Sid lived in six different houses because

The owners on Aristotle Street didn't know about each other because

Sid was taken to the vet because

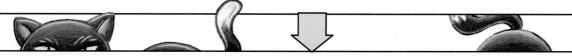

The vet called the six owners because

Sid moved to Pythagoras Place because

"Six-Dinner Sid" is about a cat who _____

_____

Name_____

Read each sentence. Write the word or words that mean the same as the numeral.

ONE TWO THREE FOUR FIVE SIX SEVEN EIGHT NINE TEN ELEVEN TWELVE

1. Sid looked at 7 neighborhoods before he found one he liked. _____

2. He enjoyed going in and out of the 18 doors and windows. _____

3. Sid never missed his 35-minute nap on Mrs. Pimm's front step. _____

4. But then his owners said that 42 meals a week were too much! _____

5. Sid walked for 56 minutes until he found a nice new neighborhood. _____

Play a game with a partner. Write down a number, using words. Cover it up. Your partner tries to guess your number by asking three questions, like "Is it between 20 and 30?"

Name _____

A. Write proper nouns to answer the questions.

July						
Sunday	Monday	Tuesday	Wednesday	Thursday	Friday	Saturday
1	2	3	Independence Day 4	5	6	7

1. What day follows Tuesday? _____

2. What month comes before September? _____

3. What day comes before Sunday? _____

4. What holiday is celebrated in July? _____

5. What holiday falls on January 1st? _____

6. What holiday is your favorite? _____

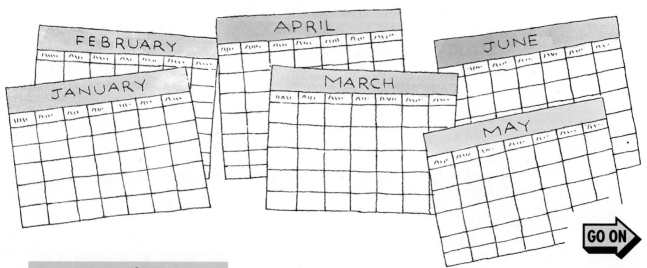

GO ON

Name_____

B. Write each sentence correctly. Add capital letters where they are needed.

7. On monday, my cat ate cereal.

_____

8. What did you feed Domino in june?

_____

9. She gets a treat on thanksgiving.

_____

10. She gets fish on sundays and thursdays.

_____

11. In february, on valentine's day, she drinks cream.

_____

Names of Days,
Months, and Holidays

Name_____

Read each sentence and the words below it.
Write the word that has the number of syllables
shown in the ( ) at the end of the sentence.

1. Our neighbors have a new _____. (2)

cat   puppy   dog

2. She is white and _____, and her name is Snowball. (2)

soft   cute   fluffy

3. She barks at all the _____ who walk by. (2)

boys   girls   grown-ups

4. Snowball has a bright red _____. (1)

leash   collar   balloon

5. One day, I took Snowball for a walk in the _____. (1)

park   city   playground

6. She ran so fast that I lost my _____.(3)

hat   coat   umbrella

With a partner, think of five other names for the puppy.
How many syllables does each name have?

Name_____

Which sentences might be the thoughts of people on Aristotle Street? Which might be the thoughts of people at Pythagoras Place? Write the sentences where they belong on the chart.

What the People on Aristotle Street Think	**What the People at Pythagoras Place Think**

SUMMARIZING
the **L**EARNING   When I classify, I put together thoughts and

ideas that are _____.

Name_____

Read each story part. Then write one sentence telling the most important idea from that story part.

1. After Sid moved away, the people on Aristotle Street missed him. The woman at number one thought, "I wish I had my sweet cat back." The man at number two thought, "I wish I were scratching that nice cat now." The people at numbers three, four, five, and six thought, "I wonder how my cat is."

   All along Aristotle Street, people asked, "Where is my cat?" Everyone felt lonely.

   _____

   _____

2. The people on Aristotle Street thought about getting new pets. The man at number three thought, "I could get a big dog." Then he shook his head. "Oh, no. A dog would make too much noise." The man at number four thought, "I will get some birds." Then he shook his head. "Oh, no. Taking care of birds is too much trouble."

   Everyone on Aristotle Street wanted a pet. After Sid, though, no other pet seemed just right.

   _____

   _____

GO ON

Name_____

3. Then the woman at number six Aristotle Street had an idea. "I'll get a cat," she said to herself. "That's it! I will get a new cat."

She told all her neighbors. "What a good idea!" they said. "I think I'll get a new cat, too."

Then the people on Aristotle Street looked at each other. "Should we really get six new cats?"

"I don't think we really need six cats," said one woman. "What we need is just one cat."

"Yes," said all the people on Aristotle Street. "This time we can share one cat."

_____

_____

Think about the important ideas you wrote. Put them together in your mind. Then write a sentence that tells the main idea of the whole story.

_____

_____

• •

SUMMARIZING *the* **L**EARNING   Put together the important ideas from the parts of

a story to tell the _____ of the whole story.

Name_____

Read each sentence and the words below it.
Write the word that best completes the sentence.

1. A family _____ into town. They go to a meeting.
   makes   marks   moves

2. _____ and gentlemen, our park is in trouble.
   Ladders   Ladies   Learning

3. This dirty park is a _____ to us all.
   dislike   disgrace   dust

4. We should make _____ to clean up the park.
   plants   plans   planets

5. Everyone _____ to pick up the trash.
   decided   deck   dinner

6. _____ can stop us from making the park beautiful!
   Not   Next   Nothing

Name_____

Fill in this chart about what happened in "Old Henry."

Who?	Old Henry; the neighbors
Where?	the neighborhood
Problem?	
Attempted Solutions?	
Effects?	
Ending?	

Write a sentence that tells the main idea of "Old Henry."

_____

_____

Name_____

Read each sentence. Correct and write the name of the month or the abbreviation of the month name you see below the line.

1. Dad gave me a diary in _____ .
                              december

2. I started writing in it in _____ .
                                january

3. I wrote the date at the top of the first page —

     _____ 1.
        jan

4. I wrote in the diary every day until _____ .
                                          march

5. In _____ , I wrote about being in a parade.
         april

6. In _____ , I started writing in my diary once a week.
         may

7. The last entry is dated _____ 12.
                               aug

Name_____

Read each sentence. Write the book title. Add capital letters where they are needed. Don't forget to underline.

Books To Read
Arthur's Pet Business
Matthew and Tilly
Jamaica Tag-Along
Six-Dinner Sid

1. Have you read moving day in Miami?

_____

2. I liked behind the hollyhocks.

_____

3. Henry and polly move west is about two mice.

_____

4. The case of the new neighbor is an exciting book!

_____

5. I found old house, new house at the library.

_____

Name_____

Finish each sentence. Write the word you see below the line, adding the ending shown after the **+**. Remember to spell the word correctly.

1. One sunny day, some _____ sat in the park.

                      lady + es

2. A mother said, "Who could feel _____ on a day like this?"

                      worry + ed

3. "Our _____ are playing together."

      baby + es

4. Just then, two _____ ran by.

          puppy + es

5. The mothers heard excited _____ from the children.

          cry + es

6. The women _____ over to the children.

        hurry + ed

7. The children and the dogs were having fun picking _____ !

                   berry + es

Name_____

Read each sentence. Write a word from the
box to complete the sentence.

phone	laugh	know	photographs
sign	wrong	wrote	

1. I don't _____ what to do for my recycling project.

2. Eduardo painted a big _____ .

3. Tasha used her camera to take _____ .

4. Sam and Lee _____ letters to the newspaper.

5. Akiko drew a cartoon that made everyone _____ .

6. I'll _____ my aunt and talk to her about my ideas.

7. It's not _____ to ask for help, is it?

Name_____

Add lines to the poem below. Make each line rhyme with the line above it. Use words from the box, or make up your own. Use words that keep the rhythm, or beat, of the poem.

We started to play	And the moose and the dog
I met a snake	And three little kittens
And we all had fun	In her bright red hat

The Party

At the edge of the lake

_____

Next came the frog

_____

Then up walked the cat

_____

We played in the sun—

_____

Name_____

Write a word from the box to complete each sentence. Use the word that means the same as the word or word group below the line.

except	gathered	quick
joined	tunes	

1. A group of turtles _____ outside.
   got together

2. Buddy is a _____ turtle.
   fast

3. He ran out the door and _____ his friends.
   went with

4. All the turtles _____ Timmy slid down the hill.
   but

5. Timmy sang silly _____ instead!
   songs

LITTLE PENGUIN'S TALE

Name_____

Fill in the story map about "Little Penguin's Tale."

Setting	Main Character	Actions
polar world	Little Penguin	sneaks away at dawn
		slides far from home
	Traits	dances with gooney birds
	silly	
	reckless	

How the Story Ends

First ending: _____

Second ending: _____

_____

What do you like best about Little Penguin? _____

_____

_____

Name_____

Read each sentence. Look at the pictures and the words below them. Write the word that makes sense in the sentence.

1. The wind _____ hard one day.

blew   **blue**

2. Little Penguin swims far out in the _____ water.

blew   **blue**

3. His friends _____ out after him.

stair   **stare**

4. "He is somewhere in the _____," they say.

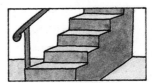
sea   **see**

5. One calls out, "I can _____ him!"

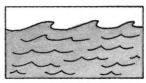
sea   **see**

6. "His _____ is sticking out of the water."

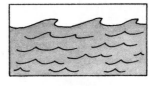
tale   **tail**

Name_____

Read each sentence. Write a noun from the ( )
to complete the sentence.

1. Kelly saw three _____.   (penguin, penguins)

2. A few _____ swam in the pool.   (seal, seals)

3. One _____ fed them fish.   (trainer, trainers)

4. Then a whale jumped over four _____.   (hoop, hoops)

5. It rang a _____, too.   (bell, bells)

Name _____

Read each sentence. Write the word that has the same vowel sound you hear in either <u>toy</u> or <u>cow</u> and that makes sense in the sentence.

toy   **cow**

1. I saw a _____ in one corner of the classroom.
   down   friend   crowd

2. Everyone was sitting _____ Mrs. Romero.
   around   with   pound

3. "Would you like to _____ us?" she asked me.
   help   coin   join

4. "We are making paper _____ ," she said.
   proud   hat   crowns

5. "Here is a sheet of _____ paper."
   yellow   town   brown

6. I asked, "_____ should I cut it?"
   Where   How   Found

7. A _____ showed me the way to cut the paper.
   boy   girl   joy

Name_____

In each pair of words, circle the word that has the same vowel sound as <u>cube</u>. Then write that word in a sentence about the picture.

cube

1. puppy mule _____

_____

2. rusty huge _____

_____

3. uses jumps _____

_____

4. cute furry _____

_____

Name_____

Read the story sentences in each picture.
Then finish the sentence beside the picture.
Write **real life** or **make-believe** on the first line.
Write your own ideas at the end of the sentence.

1.
Here are your fish!

This is from a story about _____

because _____

_____

2.
Who says penguins can't fly!

This is from a story about _____

because _____

_____

3.
Let's race through these clouds!

This is from a story about _____

because _____

_____

4.
We will be landing in New York in half an hour.

This is from a story about _____

because _____

_____

Name_____

Read each sentence and the words below it.
Write the word that best completes the sentence.

1. It was an _____ day for our neighborhood.
   important   each   inch

2. All the neighbors wanted to _____ the special day.
   cell   celebrate   brighter

3. Mr. Tien _____ us how to make party flags.
   took   taped   taught

4. Many people danced and ate at our _____.
   festive   festival   faster

5. We _____ invited the mayor to join us.
   east   every   even

Name_____

Before you read "Fiesta!" fill in the first two parts of this **KWL** chart. Write what you know and what you want to know. After you have read the story, add what you have learned.

K	W	L
What I Know	*What I Want to Know*	*What I Learned*
have picnics play games watch fireworks	How long does the celebration last? Who celebrates this holiday? What special foods do people eat?	a full day Mexicans, Mexican Americans

Write a sentence about the main idea of "Fiesta!"

_____

_____

Name_____

Read each sentence. Write a Spanish word from the box to finish the sentence.

amigo	sombrero
fiesta	taco
piñata	tortillas

We are making _____ .

I am eating a _____ .

I am wearing a _____ .

I want to break open the _____ .

He is my _____ .

We are enjoying the _____ !

Name_____

Read each sentence. Change the underlined noun to make it mean more than one. Write it on the line.

1. Fiesta visitors came on the <u>bus</u>.   _____

2. We sat on the park <u>bench</u>.   _____

3. The <u>lunch</u> looked delicious.   _____

4. We ate near the <u>bush</u>.   _____

5. We covered our <u>box</u> with paper flowers.   _____

Name _____

Read the first sentence in each pair. Think about the meaning of the underlined word. Then choose the word or words that best complete the second sentence. Write the word or words on the line.

1. We invited all our family to a party, and fifty <u>relatives</u> came.

   <u>Relatives</u> means _____ .

           family members   parties   friends

2. The family tries to get together every summer, but this was the first

   <u>reunion</u> in three years. <u>Reunion</u> means _____ .

           family   summer   get-together

3. When Aunt Lien put her Chinese dumplings on the table, Matt shouted, "Hooray! I love to eat <u>dim sum</u>." <u>Dim sum</u> means

   _____ .

     darkness   Chinese dumplings   picnic

4. Grandpa looked at the large meal on the picnic table and said,

   "What a <u>feast</u> this is!" <u>Feast</u> means _____ .

           table   good idea   large meal

SUMMARIZING *the* **L**EARNING   The other _____ in a sentence and sentences nearby can help you figure out the meaning of a new word.

Name_____

Read all of the directions carefully. Then answer the questions.

How to Make a Stick Puppet

First, get a piece of cardboard, a large craft stick, yarn, scissors, glue, a pencil, and crayons. Next, decide what character to make, and draw its shape on the cardboard. Cut out the shape. Then decorate the character. Draw its face. Glue on yarn to make hair. Add clothes. Last, glue the stick to the back of the shape. Have fun with your puppet!

1. What is the first thing you should do to make a stick puppet?

_____

_____

2. What do you do before you draw the shape of the character?

_____

3. How should you decorate the character? _____

_____

4. What is the last step? _____

SUMMARIZING the **L**EARNING

What should you do before you start to follow directions? _____

_____

••• FIESTA! •••

Name_____

Finish each sentence. Write the word you see below the line, adding the ending <u>-es</u> or <u>-ed</u>. Remember to spell the word correctly.

1. The bears had a picnic, and all the _____ went along.
   baby

2. The bears saw many _____ in the pond.
   guppy

3. They heard many _____ buzzing in the air.
   fly

4. The bears watched some _____ running in the field.
   pony

5. A few bears _____ to jump over the fence.
   try

6. At the end of the day, the bears _____ home to bed.
   hurry

Name_____

Read each sentence. Draw a line under the
word or word group that means the same as
the word in dark print.

1. On most days, Annie and Al stayed in their **favorite** part of the park.
   best-liked   oldest   worst

2. Yesterday they **tried** a new place.
   wanted   looked at   did try

3. They **hurried** to make a good boat.
   moved slowly   moved fast   did not move at all

4. Annie and Al found a nice, **round** leaf.
   like a circle   with many corners   with a few corners

5. They **brought** their own basket of food.
   gave money for   took along   found

Name_____

Think about "Miss Eva and the Red Balloon."
Fill in this chart to tell about the story.

Who? Miss Eva

Where? at school; at home

What happened? 1. Adam Sumner gave her a magic balloon.

        2. _____

        3. _____

        _____

        _____

        _____

How did it end? _____

        _____

        _____

Write a sentence to answer the question:

What did the red balloon do for Miss Eva?

_____

_____

Name_____

Read each sentence. Circle the compound word. Then write the two smaller words that make up the compound word.

1. Benny and his dad were sitting in their backyard.

_____   _____

2. Benny's dad was reading the newspaper.

_____   _____

3. Benny said, "Skip's doghouse is a mess!"

_____   _____

4. "Yes," said his dad. "It belongs in the junkyard."

_____   _____

5. "Oh, no," said Benny. "I can fix up the outside of it."

_____   _____

6. "I know someone who will help me," Benny told him.

_____   _____

7. "May we please use your paintbrush?" Benny asked.

_____   _____

Name_____

A. Write the noun that tells about the picture.

1. The _____ wait for the bus.
child   children

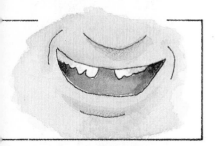

2. One girl has a missing _____.
tooth   teeth

3. The boy has his pet _____.
mouse   mice

4. He shows them to the _____.
woman   women

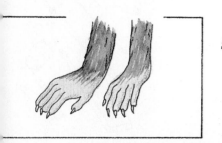

5. Mice have such tiny _____!
foot   feet

Name_____

B. The word below the line names one. Change it so that it names more than one.

6. The _____ are excited about the circus!
   child

7. Four _____ ride on prancing ponies.
   woman

8. Several _____ are dressed as circus clowns.
   man

9. What big _____ those lions have!
   tooth

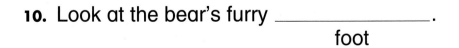

10. Look at the bear's furry _____.
    foot

Name_____

Finish each sentence. Write the word you see
below the line, adding the ending. Remember
to spell the word correctly.

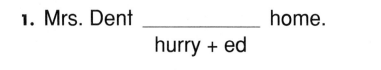

1. Mrs. Dent _____ home.
   hurry + ed

2. She _____ a big stack of books.
   carry + ed

3. She had many new _____ to read to the children.
   story + es

4. The _____ liked the books.
   baby + es

5. She showed them a picture. "Look at the _____!"
   butterfly + es

6. Juan pointed to a picture of _____.
   bunny + es

7. Rachel wanted to see pictures of _____.
   guppy + es

8. Mrs. Dent _____, but she didn't find any guppy pictures.
   try + ed

Name_____

Read about Stefan's morning. Then fill in the chart. List the things Stefan did for himself. List the things Stefan did for Sam.

Stefan's Morning

Stefan and his little brother Sam got up early. Stefan got dressed and made his bed. Then he tied Sam's shoes and helped Sam make his bed.

Stefan and Sam went into the kitchen. Stefan cracked open some nuts and gave them to Sam. Then Stefan toasted some nut bread for his own breakfast.

After breakfast, Stefan and Sam ran outside to play.

Things Stefan Did for Himself	Things Stefan Did for Sam

Name_____

Read the story. Then fill in the chart about the story. Write at least three things that could happen in real life. Write at least three things that are make-believe.

Jason's Adventure

In the middle of the night, Jason woke up and sat up in his bed. He turned on the light. He could hear music from the radio. Then his stuffed bear, Bradley, called to him, "Get up and fly with us, Jason. It's fun!"

Jason looked up. He could see Bradley and his other stuffed animals. They were all flying around the room. Jason flew up and joined them.

"This really is fun!" he shouted. They flew for two hours. Then Jason went back to bed.

The next morning, Jason's mom had to call him three times before he woke up.

Real Life	Make-Believe

Name_____

In which part of a dictionary or glossary would you find each word? Write <u>beginning</u>, <u>middle</u>, or <u>end</u> beside each word.

1. trust	_____	**2.** black	_____
3. lasso	_____	**4.** angry	_____
5. mystery	_____	**6.** wreck	_____
7. canoe	_____	**8.** yard	_____
9. dimple	_____	**10.** leek	_____

Read the words in the box. These are entry words on a dictionary or glossary page. Write the words in alphabetical order. Then circle the two guide words for that page.

bunk	bald	army	bologna
clover	airport	boil	cloak

11. _____	**12.** _____
13. _____	**14.** _____
15. _____	**16.** _____
17. _____	**18.** _____

GO ON

Name_____

Read the glossary page below. Then answer
the questions.

remember			secret
R			**S**

re·mem·ber To think about something
again: I *remember* when I
was five years old and rode a
bike for the first time.

search To try to find something:
Roberto and I will *search* for
my lost dime in the grass.

re·pair To fix: Lin will *repair* the
broken cup with glue.
syn. mend

se·cret Something a person knows
or has and does not want
anyone to know about: I can't
show you what is in my
pocket because it is a *secret*.

round Shaped like a circle or a ball:
A beach ball is *round*.

1. What are the guide words on this page? _____

2. What is the third entry word? _____

3. What does <u>search</u> mean? _____

4. What does <u>repair</u> mean? _____

5. Which word means "to think about something again"? _____

6. What is another word that could be on this page? _____

SUMMARIZING
the **L**EARNING   The words in a dictionary and a glossary are in

_____ order.